Winning with PRIDE

Personal Responsibility In Developing Excellence

By

Donny Ingram

IMG
INGRAM MANAGEMENT GROUP

ISBN: 978-1-59872-840-8

Cover design by Matt Owens
Threefolddesign.com

Editing & Proofing by Mara Burk

Printed in the United States of America
By instantpublisher.com

DEDICATION

This book is dedicated to my family, the heartbeat of my life:

Charlotte
Best friend, wife, partner,
lover, godly mother and Nana

Brad
Firstborn son, creative musician,
anointed worship leader, man of God,
faithful husband and father

Joshua
Loyal son, gifted singer,
bold witness and loving husband

Tyler
Youngest son, creative teacher,
talented musician and recording artist

FORWARD

I had the privilege of first meeting Donny Ingram in 1997 when I was searching for someone to assist me in the development and execution of a sales program for Regions Insurance. Our organization was a subsidiary of Regions Bank and we were experiencing explosive growth as the bank expanded from 10 Billion in assets in the 90's to 140 Billion in assets in 2006 and became the 10th largest bank in the country.

The challenge was to find someone who could not only handle change themselves but who had the ability to lead others in accepting what was to be monumental changes in the Banking and Insurance world. In a very short time our partners in the banks had to go from local control to centralized control, change from manual systems to computerized systems and from being "Bankers" to "Sales People" if they wanted to survive and succeed in their jobs. The reason most of our Bankers became Bankers was that they did not want to be sales people.

As the growth has shown we have obviously succeeded in our challenge and Donny was a major player in that successful transition. He developed and employed the concepts that he delivers to you in "Winning with PRIDE" in a live, ever changing and very challenging laboratory of real life. The stresses on the people he worked with were enormous and at times almost debilitating but many of them will tell you today that the only reason they survived and are now exceeding their goals, personally and professionally, was because of the training, leadership and inspiration that Donny provided them.

His life and the way he lives each day is an inspiration to all of us that know him up close and personal. I consider it an honor to be known as a friend of someone who walks the walk as well as talks the talk in every facet of this life.

Jim Taylor, CIC, CLU, ChFC
Former President of Regions Insurance (Retired)

INDEX

The Beginning of a Journey

It was 9:15 on Thursday evening December 8, 1988, when our flight landed at the Royal Jordanian Airport near Amman, Jordan. As we departed the airplane, tensions were high, we were very nervous and didn't know exactly what to expect. I had traveled to this part of the country several times as a member of the United States Air Force assigned to Central Command in Tampa, Florida, but this was my first trip traveling commercially through airports with my family. I was now a member of a Foreign Military Sales Team assigned to the American Embassy in Amman, Jordan.

My wife, Charlotte, remembered the smell of my clothes when I would return from my trips to this part of the world. The closer we came to the terminal entrance the stronger that smell became. The smell brought back memories of previous trips that were not so pleasant. When we stepped into the terminal the first thing we encountered was people sleeping everywhere, in every corner and down both sides of the walkway. Exhausted from the thirty-six hour trip with three small children, Charlotte looked at me and immediately said, "I'm going home, book me a flight now I'm taking the kids and leaving here." She felt the same as I had every time I visited this part of the world. The tension in the air was extremely heavy. Almost everyone in the terminal looked angry and upset.

As we entered the customs area we were met by my counterpart from the American Embassy. He was there to assist us in getting from the airport to downtown Amman, where we were to stay. He was excited to see us, as he should have been, because I was his replacement! He and his family were scheduled to depart in two days to return to the United States. He asked if we wanted to stay at the Intercontinental Hotel across from the American Embassy or go to our house which had been prepared for our arrival. He said it was recommended that we go to the hotel, but we chose to go to the house. I talked Charlotte into staying the weekend and promised, if she still wanted to return to the United States on Monday, I would make the arrangements and send her and the boys back home. She agreed, and off to Amman we went.

When we drove up to the front of the house, Charlotte looked at me and said, "I think I'll stay for a while." The house was beautiful. It was very large with an iron gate opening to a marble walkway leading up to the front door. The entire place was enclosed by an eight foot brick wall with iron fencing on top. It was magnificent, to say the least. It had over 3,600 square feet of living space with maid's quarters downstairs and a sun porch that was gorgeous. It was furnished with new cherry furniture and a tremendous master suite called a safe-haven. This safe-haven had a bullet proof door and steel shutters that rolled down over the windows for protection. This began an experience we would never forget, and one that would shape the remainder of our lives.

Many years later, as Charlotte and I sat drinking coffee in our den, reminiscing about the past, she asked, "How did we get where we are today?" Before I could answer, she continued, "What changed our lives, why are we so blessed?" Her questions made me stop and examine the past and evaluate our journey from the very beginning.

As we reflected, we began to remember people, events and books that helped us discover how to enjoy life by simply taking personal responsibility in developing excellence (PRIDE) in every area of our lives. It really started when we entered the United States Air Force.

2

Throughout my career, I was assigned to work for and with individuals who continually exibited excellence. It wasn't just in the performance of their Air Force duties; it was in every aspect of their life. They truly lived the Air Force core values of integrity first, service before self, and excellence in all we do. As I began to try and create the same for myself, I realized that it was a battle to do things right. That's when I recognized there is a war going on, not just in the physical realm, but within our soul also. Living and working with integrity, honesty, commitment, and care was not easy. There seemed to always be an opportunity to hide, cover up, or destroy things or information that would seemingly make life easier, look better, or avoid embarrassment. I soon realized that what appeared to be the easy way was not always the best way, but by taking personal responsibility in developing habits that lead to proper results, made life work for me as it did for those I respected and admired.

This book contains a few of our experiences and outlines principles that have assisted thousands of people in living more successful and peaceful lives. The principles of choice, design, standards, purpose, communication, attitude, and goal setting are the major reason we have been able to live life to its fullest and even overcome situations and circumstances that many would describe as insufferable. These principles provide the way to joy, contentment, and peace. They are helping us continue to learn and enjoy our journey through this life, and they will work for anyone willing to put them into practice. Everyone wants to be successful, but few are being taught that success is a by-product of excellence. By taking personal responsibility in developing excellence with the principles outlined in the pages of this book, you can expect to achieve a life of influence, respect, accomplishment and significance.

3

DECISION MAKING

1

DECISION MAKING

"The Principle of Choice"

As with most young people growing up in America, I had no knowledge of specific principles and laws in life that could ensure someone of achieving their goals, living successfully, and even surviving life threatening ordeals. Today, I see these principles being practiced by thousands of people around the world. Many are chief executive officers of major corporations, business owners, entrepreneurs, pastors, government leaders, and families who have discovered that each principle will work one hundred percent of the time when put into practice. But you must choose to use them.

In our formative years, many choices are made for us by parents, teachers, coaches, and other authoritarian figures. As we grow and become more experienced we begin to make more and more decisions on our own. Each choice is important and can have a profound effect on the future. Some people say they are where they are today because of decisions made by other people such as family, friends, teachers, or supervisors. However, blaming others will not change your future. In Victor Hugo's play, *Les Misérables*, there's a line regarding the priest Myriel, who "was fated to undergo the lot of every newcomer to a little town where there were many mouths that speak, but few heads that think." The undisciplined mind becomes a lazy mind. This is dangerous because it easily succumbs to the culture and influences around it. Taking action to make better choices will open up new avenues for achievement. The principle of choice is vital, and each person must take personal responsibility to improve their decision making ability.

According to the opinions of teachers, friends, and even some family members, I was destined to fail at most things in life. My limitations were already set, not only in their mind, but also in my own mind. I graduated high school in the half of the class that made the first half possible. I finished with only a sixth grade reading level which did not allow for a great deal of quality career choices. Furthering my education was definitely out of the question. To this day it is hard for me to understand how anyone could finish high school with such poor reading ability.

I grew up in a home where all the decisions were made according to limited understanding and focused expectations. My father was a small business owner who was excellent at his craft of building furniture. However, I did not have his talent with woodwork and after trying several jobs, I found myself married to a wonderful woman but in desperate need of a career with a promising future.

After a short time, I decided to try joining the United States Air Force. I took the entrance exam and much to my surprise I passed with flying colors, the highest score being in the field of electronics. I can't imagine how that happened, but after discussions with Charlotte, I enlisted and our life was changed dramatically from that day forward.

The decision that began to totally alter my future was actually encouraged by my first supervisor shortly after arriving at our first duty assignment at Tyndall Air Force Base in Panama City, Florida. He sold me on the idea of attending a reading lab for four hours each day until my speed and comprehension reached a 12th grade level. He was the first to teach me how to lead others by helping them see the desired end result instead of the difficulty in the journey. Being able to read better allowed me to open avenues in my mind that changed my perception of how my world could develop. Making decisions took on a new meaning, and from then on our decisions have been based on what we know to be sound principles that produce results. Don't get me wrong, I have made many bad choices through the years, but at some point I have been able to correct them and move on. I now know how important making good decisions can be in living life to its fullest, and to being able to fulfill your dreams.

I was told early in my career that "God gave us two ends, one to think with and one to sit on, and our success in life will be determined by which one we use the most." While I found this statement to be quite humorous, it made me think about the reality of its meaning; we all have choices in life and the decisions we make will determine where we go.

Every decision is important. The decision to get married, join the United States Air Force, move to Florida, and go back to school all proved to be vitally important to my future and the future of my family. However, the small decisions such as where to attend church, what automobile to purchase, what neighborhood to live in, what books to read, what movies to watch, who to create relationships with, or what clothes to wear also have long-term effects. Therefore, every decision becomes important to our future.

In the book, *The Three Spanish Philosophers,* by Jose Ferrater Mora, we're reminded by Jose Ortega y Gasset that we human beings are the only creatures on the planet that are born with the ability to choose. All the other creatures are born and guided by what we know as instinct, of which they are unaware, and do not have the capacity to question or change. For example, bears hibernate in the winter, salmon

7

swim up-stream, and geese fly south. But you and I, as human creatures, are given the power to create our own future and success. We do exactly that every day of our lives. We put into place actions and ideas that will determine the shape and form of our future.

For some these actions and ideas lead to great achievements and rewards. They end life as Zig Ziglar says, "With most of the things money will buy and all the things money won't buy." But for others, it tends to lead to a kind of humdrum life, with a lot of ups and downs, never really grabbing success and hanging on to it. The actions and ideas for many lead them to a life of frustration and problems. They spend their lives in the bottom layers of society, broke, busted, disgusted, angry, frustrated, and many even die an early death all because of choices they have made.

John Maxwell says, "We are a sum total of all the choices we've made in the past." I know for myself, I can look back over my life and clearly see that if I had made different choices my life could and probably would be very different today. When Charlotte and I decided to join the Air Force we thought it would be only four years and we would return to our home town. It actually turned out to be 21 years and the launching pad for our life purpose. Each assignment gave us a deeper understanding of life principles.

It is hard to imagine when we are making decisions, that things we think are so insignificant can have such a profound effect on our future. It is like sailing a ship across the ocean. If you make a one degree turn the second day out of the docks, no one notices, but a week or two later you will discover that you are way off course and much is required to correct your direction. However, we can't cry over spilled milk can we? It does not matter where we are now. Each of us must start making better choices today. We must judge every decision we make on how it could possibly affect our future.

The decision to take my family to Jordan with me had a life-long effect on the entire family. Being there and

8

having to live under what most Americans would call primitive circumstances, made us appreciate more of the little things we have today such as drinking water from the kitchen sink. Compared to third world countries, America has pure drinking water. It is not contaminated with amoebas and germs that can cause sickness and even death.

Being able to follow the historical facts in the Bible became a pastime for our family. Today when the boys hear or read about Biblical places and events such as Mount Nebo, where Moses viewed the promise land, they can picture it clearly in their mind because we have visited that location many times. Those opportunities have proven to be priceless in our life.

One can never know the impact of an opportunity until taking advantage of it. Shortly after we arrived in Amman, Jordon, I was offered the opportunity to coach one of the Junior Basketball teams. My oldest son, Brad, wanted to play. I knew I would be there everyday anyway, and even though I was apprehensive because of the language barrier with the players, I chose to accept the opportunity. Then, I met my assistant coach who was Egyptian and could not speak English. What a time we had trying to communicate with each other and to the kids at the same time. Even though it was a challenge for me, we had a great time and it made me a much better communicator by accepting the opportunity.

My middle son, Josh, was also playing on a younger team. At the end of his season, we were watching his final game when something happened that tested my decision-making ability. They were playing a team whose coach was a little hyper, to say the least. The game was close and the other team's coach came running down the side lines and shoved Charlotte as he went past. Well, me being a southern gentleman, I could not let this go unnoticed. I reached out and grabbed his shirt and spun him around. As I went to ask him what he was doing, he began swinging at me. Several of the men standing on the sidelines grabbed hold of us both

9

before it went too far. I was furious, I was so mad I was shaking. He was yelling something at me in Arabic and I wanted so badly to retaliate. I know I said far more than I should have, but fortunately I knew better than to act on my emotions. At that moment, you could hear a pin drop. Everyone became quiet as a mouse. There was so much tension in the air, the wrong move could have brought about disaster. I have found that many times when a challenging opportunity comes along, there is always some situation or circumstance that arises that can spoil any future possibilities. We must identify them quickly and prevent the urge to continue.

After a short period of time, we began to cool down. Charlotte encouraged me not to cause an international incident. After the game, I experienced my first Arabic apology when the man who shoved her came over and kissed me on both cheeks as his way of saying, "I'm sorry." He refused to apologize to Charlotte, but I understood why and I acknowledged forgiveness, and away we went.

1989
Meeting with King Hussein bin Talal of Jordan

The opportunity to coach the junior basketball team opened many more interesting events. One such occasion was coaching the Jordanian Little League All-Star baseball team representing Jordan in the European tournaments. This opened a door to being invited to the Palace to meet with King Hussein bin Talal of Jordan for an introduction of the team. He gave each of us a beautiful watch with his name engraved on the face and wished us well in the tournaments.

I still have this picture hanging in my office with the King in the palace which made the front page of the Jordanian Times. That picture has aroused many discussions which, in turn, opened the door to more opportunities than I could have ever expected. What an experience!

Sometimes it is hard to imagine where an opportunity will take you. But it is important to realize that success or failure as a human being is not a matter of luck or circumstance. It is not a matter of fate, or the breaks, who you know, or any of the other myths and clichés many use as an excuse. It is, however, a matter of following the PRIDE principles and using the guidelines that are simple. When we follow such principles and guidelines, we can create the change we want to see in ourselves. We can create more of the moments in life that matter. We can experience all that life has to offer if we make the right choices, and it's never too late to start.

I believe the one choice that helps most people achieve a balanced success in life is their faith or spiritual belief, which influences decision making. Your belief system will determine your values, and your values will help dictate the choices you make in life. What I mean by "balanced success" is being successful in every area of your life; physically, professionally, financially, mentally, educationally, with family, faith, and community. Many have success in a few of these areas, but after thirty-one years of traveling and working around the world, my study and personal observations indicate that only those who live

11

what they *truly believe* actually achieve the level of success they desire, which is a level others can only dream about. I've learned that all behavior is driven by belief, which means that your belief determines your behavior or action, and your actions will determine your destiny. Therefore, where you go, what you do, and what you achieve all depends on how or what you believe. Today many people have rejected the beliefs and values of their forefathers and try to establish beliefs for themselves that have no foundation and no track record for success. The principles I am talking about in this book have been proven over hundreds of years, and they will work for anyone willing to take personal responsibility in putting them into practice.

Traveling to foreign countries, especially Third World countries, is where I began to understand the power of spiritual beliefs. In many cultures people are taught to believe in false truths, pagan gods, and unrealistic expectations. I've seen everything from worshiping the sun, to worshiping cows, statues, carvings, buildings, and people who never existed, or who no longer exist. People believe in things like reincarnation, that they have lived in another life and will live again after this life maybe, as a dog, cat, bird, or something even more outrageous.

For a long time, I didn't know exactly how to confront such beliefs because it is hard for anyone to imagine their cultural beliefs to be wrong; parents would never teach their children a lie. Not one person in all my travels and encounters could provide me any proof or evidence that these beliefs were based on truth. What I was able to see in my own faith and belief, that was not present in other religions, was a manifestation of my beliefs. I actually see, feel, and enjoy the fruits of my beliefs here and now. I have proof that what I experience as a result of my spiritual beliefs was stated over two thousand years ago in the best selling book of all time – the Bible.

I know there is a tremendous amount of controversy over religious beliefs, especially Christianity. Events over the years and modern science have discovered much of what was documented in the Bible by some forty authors over a period of fifteen hundred years to be true and accurate. I have always considered myself to be an open-minded individual. I will listen to almost anyone and try many things, but first I want to see proof that it is reliable and have lasting benefits for me personally. No one can prove to me that which is written in scripture to be false because I have always received the promises when I act on the principles outlined in the pages of the Bible. Of those who refuse to believe, I would ask one thing, don't knock it until you have tried it with all your heart because the principles taught in the Bible will bring the results that everyone is trying to discover through so many different methods.

I believe most anyone can have everything in life they want, if they are willing to make the commitment and sacrifices needed to get it. We can be that energetic individual we long to be. We can all get up every morning with total passion for living. We can be that joyful creative person, we can have that healthy fit body we desire and we can be the influence on our family and friends they need. We _can_! The problem is our belief systems keep us from engaging the parts of us that would make it a _must_ and not a _should._

Whatever it is you want to see, do, or have has to become a _must_ in your life. I hear too many people saying, "I should do this or I should do that" and "_should_" will not make it happen. And we all have "_shoulds,_" right? I should lose weight...I should eat less...I should exercise more...etc. I heard one man say "most of the time we '_should_' all over ourselves and accomplish nothing." Whatever it is you want to see happen, has to become a "must" in your life or you will never experience the reality of it.

How do we do that? The first step is defining why you want it. The why must be powerful or you will never

13

make it a must. For most people it is a pain/pleasure principle. You either find it too painful not to achieve, or so pleasurable you must achieve it. This principle is why many never make the decision to be great, do the extraordinary, or have certain things in life. Smoking for example, even though the package is stamped with a warning that cigarettes will cause cancer, people still smoke because they do not see an immediate danger, no instant pain. They reason to themselves that they can "always" quit. If they thought by smoking a cigarette they would develop cancer immediately, no one would ever start.

Make the things you want to accomplish in life a must by engaging your belief system. Base your beliefs on truth, not on false facts and opinions of people who have no proof that their beliefs will become reality. When you do, you will begin to make better quality decisions. Remember what author and consultant Brain Tracy says, "What the mind can conceive and believe can be obtained," but it should be based on truth. Then document the goals you want to achieve, define why you want them, set an action plan, and measure yourself continually to know where you are and how you are progressing and success will be inevitable.

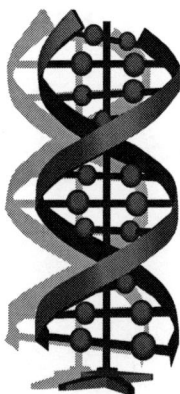

DNA

FUNCTIONING PHYSICALLY

2

FUNCTIONING PHYSICALLY

"The Principle of Design"

Years ago, Lloyds of London, a large European insurance company, conducted a study that resulted in some fascinating results. There have been several studies since this study that documented the same outcome, but I like how the Lloyds study reported their findings. One of the interesting things revealed was when a man gets a kiss from his wife before going to work and after coming home (not a peck on the check but a real lip-lock or as those in Alabama would say, "a wet-one") earned an average of 25% more money and lived five and one half years longer than the man who did not get a kiss.

My question was, "How could this be?" What could it be about a kiss that would cause a man to earn more and live longer? Let me explain what I learned. When a man receives a kiss like that, he feels secure, confident, needed, loved and significant, it makes him feel good! Therefore, when he goes into the workplace he produces more, he is more creative, he gets the promotions, he gets the raises and bonuses, he gets the contracts, etc. When a person feels confident and significant, they live at a different level than those who don't. Therefore, they make better quality decisions and their life improves.

One of the most important principles to understand is one of design. We must begin to recognize that as a human we are specifically designed to succeed and win in life. Our creator made us in such a unique way that winning in life may not be easy, but it can be simple. The problem is, over the years we have allowed so many influences to infiltrate our minds and lives that we have forgotten, and even rejected, the real factors of human behavior and success.

I really believe what the Bible says about us as humans, *"we are fearfully and wonderfully made."* Even our body is designed to succeed. When you get a bruise, puncture, or break, your body begins immediately to heal itself. It will fight any foreign bacteria, it heals itself from within, and it regenerates and creates the chemicals necessary to sustain life. This is a great example to help us understand where success starts -- on the inside.

Today, more people are taking mind-numbing/mood-altering drugs than anytime in history. It is terrifying to think that so many people are putting a foreign substance or chemical inside their body to get a feeling that most could enjoy if they would only take the actions necessary to start the natural chemicals working. I am not a doctor or psychologist, but I have read the studies, questioned the experts, and experienced what I am telling you. Medical science has proven we have the ability to get the feeling we want, when we want it. Don't get me wrong, some people need serious medical attention and help getting their body in balance, the rest of us can do it ourselves if we would only try.

Think about how your feelings change when you see a movie, maybe one that makes you cry or an action movie that excites you. Why do your feelings change so rapidly? You have taken an action to view and listen to something that your brain responded to and began to produce the chemicals/hormones/endorphins that give you that feeling. That is the beauty of how you were designed. You are in control of how you feel. It is true that when we hear, smell,

17

taste, see, or touch something our mind is stimulated to respond in some way.

This is why music is so powerful. Let me give you an example of what I am talking about. Have you ever noticed that many of the department stores where you shop have music playing in the background? They know from studies and experience that music affects the moods of shoppers, and in most cases it puts them into a higher state of awareness. I read a few years ago where one company said if a retail store would allow their music to be played in the store they would guarantee a 25% increase in sales or the service would not cost the retailer a cent. How can they make such an offer? Because they know the power of listening to the right music can cause the human brain to respond, hence, people purchase more.

Music became a vital part of our life while living in the Middle East. The prayers that blared loudly five times each day from every mosque in the city was irritating and not very pleasing to our ears. In fact, every time we heard it we became tense, uneasy, and annoyed. Even though it was an encouragement and necessity to the native Muslims, it did not do anything for us. We were able to overcome that feeling by doing what medical researchers say will help change the way you feel, listen to something that is uplifting, inspiring or motivating. What this actually does is jump start the production of serotonin by the brain, which is necessary for how well we feel and function.

Two things did it for us, music and prayer. We could listen to certain music or we would pray in our own understanding, according to our beliefs and instantly feel better. This happened because we initiated something that our brain responded to, and thus produced the chemicals necessary in helping us achieve the feeling we desired.

Our brain responds to everything we do. A study documented by the Institute in Basic Life Principles revealed that when you smile your brain releases a hormone that strengthens your immune system. It also revealed when you frown a hormone is released that weakens your immune system. The researchers took it one step further and proved that when you see someone smile or frown that same hormone is released in you. It is sometimes the little things we overlook that mean the most to us as humans, especially in regard to our health. The scriptures bare this out in Proverbs chapter 17 verse 22, where it says, "*A merry heart doeth good like a medicine.*"

It is time we understand how our body functions, especially our brain, and start using what we have been equipped with in order to begin living at a higher standard and enjoying more of this life than ever before. Start listening to things that will inspire, uplift, and motivate you. When you do, it will ignite the things inside that cause more positive feelings, which in turn leads to better decisions, improved health and a more prosperous life.

WINNING

3

WINNING

"The Principle of Standards"

One of the most important tools to influencing the quality of your life is the standards by which you live, work, and play. The first thing that comes to mind when I think of standards is the people we surround ourselves with. I have learned that the people I create a relationship with and hang around will determine, to a great extent, where I go in life and what I am able to accomplish. The hardest thing to get young people to realize is that who they associate with will be who they become. If people have a lower standard than you, you will be prone to lower your standards for them. Especially if it is someone you care about.

First let me say that people come into your life for a *reason*, a *season* or a *lifetime*. When someone is in your life for a *reason*, it is usually to meet a need you have expressed. They have come to assist you through a difficulty, to provide you with guidance and support, to aid you physically, emotionally or spiritually. They may seem like a godsend and many are. They are there for the reason you need them to be. Then, without any wrongdoing on your part or at an inconvenient time, this person will say or do something to bring the relationship to an end. Sometimes they die and sometimes they walk away. Sometimes they act up and force you to take a stand. What we must realize is that our need

21

has been met, our desire fulfilled, their work is done. The prayer you sent up has been answered and now it is time to move on.

Some people come into your life for a *season*, because your turn has come to share, grow or learn. They bring you an experience of peace or make you laugh. They may teach you something you have never done. They usually give you an unbelievable amount of joy. But it's only for a season. *Lifetime* relationships are the ones that teach you lifetime lessons, things you must build upon in order to have a solid emotional foundation. Your job is to accept the lesson, love the person and put what you have learned to use in all other relationships and areas of your life.

When you can identify why someone comes into your life, which is not always easy, you will know what to do and how to respond to that person. That's important because most people's lives are a direct reflection of their peer group. Meaning – what your peers think or feel affects you, and your life will reflect that. What happens if you have a higher expectation and standard than your peer group? They may try and pull you down to their level. Not that they want to hold you back but they fear losing you. If you give in and lower your standards to theirs you will never achieve the level of success you were meant to achieve. It's the old adage "If you lay down with dogs you'll get up with fleas." You deserve better, so hold out for it. It may mean some people in relationship with you will walk away, so be it. Sometimes you have to give up less in order to have more.

It takes courage to break the mold and step outside the boundaries others create for you. When you do, you will face criticism. Just remember, insecure people will always criticize you, especially if your choices differ from theirs. That is because they are uncomfortable with things that do not conform to their way of thinking. Secure people can handle being the only one doing something. Remember that there are two kinds of people who always fail – those who listen to nobody and those who listen to everybody.

Too often our actions are dictated not by a sense of purpose, but by a need to please. We sometimes care so much about what certain people think that, with every step, we look over our shoulder to see whether they are smiling or frowning. Determine and hold to your standards. Encourage your peers and friends to raise their standards. If they have the desire and will, they will come up with you. If not, they will fade away, which is alright. It doesn't mean you do not care about them, but you must determine what you are after and commit to get there.

During my years at Maxwell Air Force Base, while working for Air University, I encountered a young man who was one of those characters with whom nothing ever went right. Almost everyday, without fail, he would be late for work. He seemed to be depressed and unhappy with everything in his life. I tried for months to get him to see that one of his problems was his outlook, the low standards he had. One day, my supervisor, who I valued as a good friend, relayed to me some startling observations. He said, "Donny, you're allowing Billy's negative outlook on life to affect your outlook, and your goals, don't lower yourself to his standards."

I was stunned. At first I didn't believe it, but then it hit me, I must stick to my standards and stop allowing him to affect me in a negative way. At that moment, I made a decision to change. The very next day, I called him into my office and very calmly and positively explained what we were experiencing and what must change. I gave him no room to maneuver and get away with continuing to set low standards for himself.

It didn't turn around at that moment, but day after day, I refused to allow him to even continue his negative conversations or express his bad feelings. It was easy for me to do this, because I was his supervisor. After several months, he stopped trying to talk negatively about anything.

23

He even began to have creative comments about our work projects and the things we were trying to accomplish. His ideas were great and everyone reinforced his creative thinking with their positive comments about him and his abilities. In short, Billy began to see himself differently, and he began to set higher standards for himself.

Many years later, after our careers had gone separate ways; I received a phone call from him. He was in the area and wanted to have lunch with me. At that lunch I saw a very different man than the one that worked for me so many years earlier. He was confident, bold, and creative; he had a vision, a purpose and passion. He had been promoted several times and was looking forward to everyday. What a difference setting the proper standards can make!!!

Sounds simple, but its true! If you want more today than yesterday, you must raise your standards to get there. It doesn't matter where you are now, to get where you want to be and do the things you desire, and have all that life can offer, you must raise your standards.

This may be easier to see if you think of it in terms of performance and rewards. In today's corporate world what kind of rewards are given for poor performance? I used to think, poor performance will equal poor rewards, but that is not true. Poor performance today will get you the "pink slip;" it will get you down-sized, out-sourced, or right-sized. Most of us work in a results-orientated environment, and there is no acknowledgement for anyone performing poorly.

What can be expected for good performance? Like many people, I thought good performance equaled good rewards, but that is not true, either. Good performance will get you poor rewards. This is the standard most people live and work at today. I hear people say, "I've been a good husband, why did my wife have an affair?" "I've been a good wife, why did my husband leave me?" "We've been good parents, why are our kids on drugs or in jail?" It is sad to tell them but they answered their own question. Good performance in life, as well as work, gets you poor rewards.

24

Let's take it higher than "good" and ask what kind of rewards are available for those whose performance is excellent? I believe you will find that the rewards are excellent for people performing with excellence. This should be the standard we strive for every day.

See yourself for who you really are!

I remember several years ago I was watching an NBA championship game on television. After the game, a reporter asked the MVP, "What makes you so good?" His response was that he played with the same philosophy as another NBA player whom he had watched and admired as a youngster. His philosophy was, "Everyday I go out on the court, I demand more of myself than anyone else could possibly ask." He explained that this PRIDE principle is what made him the player he is.

I thought to myself, what would happen if we all set a standard of excellence everyday. What reward could we expect if every morning we determined excellence is our standard? If I said, "Today I'm going to be a better spouse than my husband or wife could every dream of; I'm going to be a better parent than my children could every hope for; I'm going to be a better employee than my company could ever afford to hire." What could be achieved if we set excellence as our daily standard?

The rewards at this level are excellent as this MVP explained. Performing at an excellent level at work and in life will lead to excellent rewards. Rewards that only a few achieve and others only dream about.

I want to ask another important question. What really determines your quality of life? I have met some who think the weather will help determine it; others say relationships, and most everyone will say for sure money. In reality it is none of these. These are external entities/environments that far too many people allow to control their feelings. There are lots of people with money who are still unhappy. Money won't change who you are, it will only intensify who you are. If you are a pain and you get money, you'll just have more to be a pain with. Only one thing determines how you feel and that is the way you communicate with yourself.

The most important person you can talk to every day is yourself. Don't expect other people to believe you are skilled, talented, beautiful, sexy and successful until you believe it. The problem is you will not believe it until you start telling yourself. You need to get up every morning, look at yourself in the mirror, and make a proclamation for what you want to see in your life.

There are many people who have been through terrible physical, sexual, or financial traumas, and their lives have turned out great. Why? They communicate to themselves in a positive manner. They look for the good in everything and everyone. The great steel tycoon, Andrew Carnegie, once said "Your world begins to change when you become a good-finder not a fault-finder."

Many people today and many down through history, have had serious physical disabilities; many were abused as children or raised in poverty, yet they were able to contribute tremendously to society. Some you might recognize are Franklin D. Roosevelt, Sir Winston Churchill, Clara Barton, Helen Keller, Mother Teresa, Dr. Albert Schweitzer, and Martin Luther King Jr.

Tony Robbins says in his training series *"Unleashing the Power Within,"* "It's never the things of your life that determine the quality; it is the meaning you give to those things that determine quality." He tells us that the quality of our life has nothing to do with our real life. It has everything to do with what we communicate to ourselves. What you communicate with certainty, you will believe. And when you believe it, you will feel it and whatever you feel is your life. That's what we are all after is a feeling, right? We just need to learn how to get it.

Nothing in life has any meaning except the meaning we give it. Some people can go through a situation and say to themselves, "My life is over, God hates me." Yet someone else can have the same experience and say, "I'm just being challenged to reach down deep and see who I really am." What's the difference? One is defeated and the other is driven and excited. There is nothing more important than communication to one's self. Few ever master it, but all of us are capable.

The reason we do not communicate with ourselves better is that it's not our primary focus. We're taught today that "things" are more important because "things" will provide the feeling we are seeking. So we get busy doing everything we can to obtain "stuff," thinking it will make us feel good, but the stuff will only provide the feeling for a short period of time. When the stuff doesn't give us what we want, some reach for a drug or a drink, or visit a doctor who really cares and provides what? Another drug! Even that doesn't work because we are still unhappy. Because we haven't changed the way we communicate with ourselves, maybe a little, but not one hundred percent. We still do not have the change we're after.

If you want to see a lasting, positive change, then you must set excellence as your standard and begin communicating with yourself in a more positive manner. Positive communication will change your thinking, your thinking will change your actions, and your actions will make your future brighter, healthier, and more profitable.

DIRECTION

4

DIRECTION

"The Principle of Purpose"

———————

The worst kind of life is a life without purpose, stuck in the same old routine. Tony Evans writes, "Every day you get out of the same old bed and go to the same old bathroom to look at the same old face in the same old mirror. You go to the same old closet to choose from the same old clothes, and then sit down at the same old breakfast table to eat the same old breakfast. Then you go to that same old car to head down that same old road to that same old job. There you work all day for the same old pay, next to those same old people, supervised by that same old manager. Then you get back into that same old car and head back down that same old road to that same old house. Once you are home you sit down in that same old chair to watch that same old television. At the end of the day you go to that same old bed and sleep that same old way, so you can get up the next morning and start that same old routine all over again."

You weren't created to live a purposeless existence. Even if you are searching to find your life's purpose – there's something out there worth the search! The things around you are not all there is. You must seek it, find it, and live it to the fullest! Purpose is the one thing that many fail to identify early in life. That is why Miles Monroe, author of *In Pursuit of Purpose* says, "The place you can find the most potential is the cemetery because people go to the grave and never fulfill their purpose in life." Purpose is important because it produces passion, and when you have passion about something you accomplish it.

We all want passion, but we fail to discover how to get it. I know passion sounds exciting, but before we can have passion about anything: relationship, job, life, or faith, there is something else that must be identified and that is purpose. Let me start by showing you an equation that I believe is the starting point for success in anything you attempt: Belief + Behavior = Results (B+B=R).

We are all looking for results, right? But what if we're not getting what we want? Something has to change. The thing that must change is our behavior. Remember what Einstein said, "If you want something you've never had, you must do things you've never done." We must change our behavior. This sounds simple, but it's more difficult for some than others. For a number of us, before we can change our behavior, we must change our belief. Remember, I said earlier that "all action is belief driven." Here lies the heart of our success in reaching our full potential. If we do not believe we will get the result by exhibiting the behavior, we'll never demonstrate the behavior.

There are at least eight components of our life that we must deal with. Actually there are nine, counting the core from which all others must flow, if we're going to achieve what we were designed to achieve. The eight components are all present to some degree in each of us. They are as follows: physical, professional, financial, mental, educational, family, faith, and community. Problems occur when they are not balanced. We find many who are successful in one or more but fail in the others causing frustration, divorce, stress, sickness, and in extreme cases even death.

31

Each of these areas must flow from the core, which is the spiritual component. Because our actions come from our beliefs and our beliefs come from many different areas – environment, schooling, faith, up-bringing. Whether you like it or not, believe it or not, we are spiritual beings. Denise Waitley, author of *The Physiology of Winning* said it like this, "We are not human beings having spiritual experiences. We are spiritual beings having human experiences." Our beliefs are fed into us and they form the basis for our future. Now, please understand that our beliefs can change based on experiences, education, and revelation knowledge, etc.

For example, remember September 11, 2001? What did America do when this tragedy struck? Pray! Prior to this event, prayer was not allowed in certain places. Why? Because it wasn't politically correct, or most did not believe in God, or would not admit they did. After this event, we saw everyone from the White House to daycares praying over the loss of many loved ones in New York, over the leaders of our great nation, and the war on terrorism. It seemed to be acceptable then, to go to God for protection and answers, even though it wasn't very long before we reverted back to the old way of thinking. I believe we sometimes suppress our true beliefs, and they will not be unveiled, until some tragedy strikes that causes us to reject everything and everyone, and turn to what we believe deep down to be our answer.

It is like one fellow I know who was on a Delta flight a few years ago. When the plane developed problems, the announcement came over the intercom to prepare for a crash landing. He stood and asked the question "Can I pray for our safety?" He received 100% approval and was asked to go ahead and do it quickly.

It's about time we turn back to what made this nation great. Our forefathers had purpose, courage, commitment, and passion. They sought out a new land where they could worship freely, prosper, and grow.

Their principles and values formed a great nation and allow us to still enjoy freedom in America today. I'm glad there is a point where people will begin to recognize their faith and live what they believe. You may not believe in God right now, that's alright; that's the beauty of America. At some point you must begin to have faith in a God that can answer your prayers and meet your needs. The only way I have ever seen anyone live a fulfilled, balanced life, is living what they believe. Some people believe in the craziest things. In India for example, people believe cows are sacred and most of the population lives in poverty and hunger while the ribeyes roam freely. The Hindus of India also believe the Ganges River is holy, it is a goddess. Actually it is extremely polluted by dead bodies, sewage, and chemicals from factories. I could give many more examples, but the point is, will they find the balanced, fulfilled life by believing what they do?

Living for anything other than the one true God will only leave you unfulfilled, and definitely out of balance. Only God satisfies, and having that satisfaction can only come from knowing Him. Contrary to what some believe, we are His creation made for His purpose and we must discover that purpose.

Purpose is the starting point to setting and achieving goals. Without purpose there is no passion, and having passion is the fuel you need to become the success you were designed to be. Your passion will determine your success and the success of the company where you work. Passion comes from a clearly defined purpose for your life. What are you here for? People everywhere want to know their purpose. That is why Rick Warren's book, *The Purpose Driven Life*, has sold so many copies.

Miles Monroe says, "Purpose is inherent." He says, "When a manufacturer creates a new product, he lets the product's intended use govern the design, function, and nature of the product so that the fulfillment of its purpose is inseparably built into it." The same happens when men and women are created; their Creator designs them to fulfill their function and gives them certain qualities and characteristics that enable them to perform His intended purpose. These qualities are yours before birth.

Therefore, your natural inclinations to socialize with people, to seek solitude, to think with your mind or to do things with your hands, to communicate with words or to express yourself through the various art forms, to come up with the ideas or to put them into action, to lead or to follow, to inspire or to manage, to calculate or to demonstrate are part of your makeup and your personality from the time your Creator chose to make you and design you in a particular way. They relate to your purpose, which is a natural, innate, and intimate part of who you are.

Keep in mind that it is essential that you never try to become like someone else. You can and should learn from others, but you must never try to become them. Farai Chideya graduated from Harvard, worked for *Newsweek* magazine and quickly rose to the top. Yet she spent years living in the private hell of bulimia, trying to become like the glossy images in the make-believe world around her. When she finally broke free from the destructive grip of her disease, she wrote, "Losing weight didn't change my personality and it didn't lighten the emotional baggage I carried from my childhood. I thought I wanted to be thin. What I really wanted was to be happy, and neither my looks nor my achievements could do that. Because I couldn't love or accept myself, the acceptance of others was never enough. When I tried to be perfect, I came across as remote and unapproachable, yet the exact opposite was what I wanted." You can never fulfill your purpose without being yourself. Who and what you are is important and essential to why you are.

Stop and think about yourself for a minute. Who are you, what are your desires, your beliefs, your goals and especially what do you feel your life should stand for? You may even want to write what you feel your purpose is right

34

now. Until you define your purpose in life, it will be hard to be passionate about anything.

Mike Murdock, author of several great books on our assignments in life, says your life purpose can come from something you dislike or even love very much. For example, some have become doctors because they hate to see people suffer with disease and sickness. Others have become lawyers due to some misuse they see in the justice system. Many have recognized their talents and skills and enjoyment in certain areas and used them to launch a rewarding career.

Many companies today are recognizing that purpose is extremely important to their success because purpose brings meaning to what a person is doing and how well they do it. Let me explain. There are essentially three types of companies that operate throughout the world today. You can recognize them by what their mission is. The first is profit-driven. They focus on making money, the bottom line. It doesn't matter what sign you find in the lobby for visitors to read, there is very little recognition and celebration of the human spirit in a profit-driven company. There is very little or no passion, because it's hard to get passionate about profits especially when they are generated for someone else.

The second type of company is the customer-driven organization. Here is the first glimmering of synergy, which means "together energy." These companies strive to create a sense of contribution to the customer and the employee. The energy level is significantly greater than in the profit-driven company, turn-over is lower and morale is higher.

To truly maximize the potential of every human being in the workplace, to bring out a sense of passion and commitment, there is a third level to which a successful organization must seek, that is to become a meaning-driven company. As humans you and I seek meaning. Remember this statement by Tony Robbins, I'll share more about it in a later chapter, "It's not what happens in life that produces quality of life, but it is the meaning we apply to what happens that determines the quality of life we live." Without meaning we feel insignificant, fearful, and disconnected. When we can attach meaning to what we do, we feel significant, confident, and connected to the organization as well as those around us.

A few years ago, *USA Today* printed a study conducted of over one hundred companies. In the study, the employees of each company were asked what their views and desires were for their jobs. Management was then asked their views about what the employees wanted. The results are as follows:

MANAGEMENT	EMPLOYEE
1. Good Salary	1. Interesting Work
2. Good Benefits	2. To be appreciated for their work
3. Job Security	3. A feeling of being in on things

What the employees really wanted was meaning from their job. As individuals we are ultimately responsible for assigning meaning to what we do. However, I'm not excusing parents, supervisors, managers and executives because these individuals have the power to give meaning to the people under their authority. But, it is ultimately up to you and me to find meaning in what we do.

This reminds me of a story of a man walking past a building site. As he passed he stopped and asked the first man he came to what he was doing? The worker replied with disgust, "I'm building a wall." The man was still curious so he stopped and asked a second man. This second worker replied, "I'm building a church." He was a little more forthcoming. The man went on around the corner and came to another worker that was slapping bricks along a string line with zeal. This workman was whistling cheerfully as he worked. The man asked, "What are you doing?" The third worker replied with a bright smile, "I'm building a cathedral, a place where lives will be changed. This is a building in which marriages and families will be strengthened, the bonds of addiction will be broken, missionaries will be funded and encouraged, and people will lift their hearts and their songs to heaven. The members of our community who walk in here will leave with a real sense of truth and destiny, and with a greater knowledge of our Lord of Glory."

This man was passionate about what he was doing because he gave it meaning. Jack Lannom, author of *Untapped Potential* said, "Only meaning extricates man from mediocrity and propels him into magnificence." Out of purpose comes meaning, and from meaning comes passion. The most powerful things that have consequence in your life is the decisions you make. These decisions are a result of your purpose. I stated earlier that we are the only creatures created on earth that have the ability to make choices. These choices or decisions form our future.

The first decision we all must face in any situation or circumstance is what do I focus on? Where your focus is will determine what you feel, where you go, and what you do. We must focus! The second decision is what does it mean? This is the only thing we have total control over and meaning is what forms our attitude. The last, but the most important decision, is what am I going to do?

Let me say this, "what drives you will determine your decisions." Does fear, faith, adventure, or guilt of the past drive you? Drive means to guide, control or direct. Whatever drives you will determine your life.

Anything worth living in life will require a certain amount of faith or trust. When you lose trust, you lose meaning and when you lose meaning, you lose life. Maybe not physically, but inside you die emotionally, which if not dealt with, can lead to physical death.

The Massachusetts Department of Health Education & Welfare conducted an interesting study released a few years ago. In the study they were looking for the "mind-body connection." The question they were trying to answer was, "What causes someone under age fifty to die after their first heart attack and not recover and live on." They thought the answer would be too much cholesterol in the body, diabetes, or something else that caused failure. But it was none of these. The study proved that what caused a person to die after their first heart attack was "Job Dissatisfaction." The study showed those who lived on for years after their heart attack had purpose and meaning in their life. They didn't say, "Well I'm back in the salt mines again, or I'm on the tread mill of life again." You and I must have purpose and we must decide what it is.

In 1985, I had a friend that was diagnosed with cancer and was told he would die within six months. He told the doctors, "I respect what you're telling me and I know you're looking at the facts, but only God determines when my time is up and I happen to know that I have much more to do before I'm finished on this earth. I'm going to walk out of here." He realized that facts and truth are different. He knew his purpose. He did walk out of that hospital and didn't return until 2001 when the cancer reoccurred and again the doctors told him he would die within months. This time he said, "Now I'm ready, I'm finished." I spoke at his funeral just a few months later. Wouldn't it be life giving if we all knew our purpose to this extent?

It is said that Michael Landon on his death bed stated, "I wish someone would have told me early in my life that I was dying, then I could have lived every day to its fullest." The number one reason people live without joy and fulfillment is lack of purpose. Make the choice today and decide to live your purpose. In your purpose you will find meaning and the special plan for your life.

UNDERSTANDING

5

UNDERSTANDING

"The Principle of Communication"

To be successful in life today you must be a good communicator. Success in marriage is directly related to the communication skills of the married couple. Success in the workplace is no exception. Even the meaning-driven company, with its focus on maximizing the potential of every one of their employees, will fail if good communication is not practiced. Your personal success will rise and fall in direct proportion to your communication skills with those around you. Communication skills are often taken for granted, yet taking the time to improve your communication skills will greatly help you in achieving your goals and reaching your destiny in life.

We have learned a great deal about communication in the past twenty or thirty years, but most people still do not realize the power of communication and how it can propel you into your destiny. I have learned valuable principles by reading studies and listening to men and women who have documented evidence on the power of communication. I've put into practice principles that allow me to do more than I ever dreamed possible by knowing how to communicate the right message to others and to myself.

We now know from many studies, by great institutions like the University of Southern California, that communication is not just words. Research shows that when two people meet and communicate, what actually influences one or the other to change the way they feel or act is more than mere words.

In human communication, we find that words represent only 7% of what actually influences someone to change how they feel or act toward something. As a marketer, trainer, and salesperson, I always thought if I could find the right words to say, I could influence someone to buy my product or idea. I quickly learned it takes more than words.

Greater than words are our voice qualities. Voice qualities represent 38% of what actually influences someone to change the way they feel or act. What are voice qualities? Voice qualities include tone, timber, volume, or speed with which we speak. This is really nothing new because we have known for years that it's not what you say as much as it is how you say it.

However, the thing that most influences a person to change the way they feel or act is physiology, or how we use our physical body. Most of us would say body-language. Physiology represents 55% of what actually influences someone to change. What do I mean by physiology? facial expressions, muscular tension, gestures, and posture are part of physiology.

Have you ever made a statement to someone and they responded, "Sure," but at the same time they rolled their eyes and their voice went from low to high? What were they communicating to you? That it will never happen. Why? Their words were right but their voice and physiology didn't match. Behavioral scientists say that our communication must be congruent if it is to be believable. Congruent means all three, our words, voice, and physiology must match. When they all agree, you hold the power to influence others to change the way they feel and act.

One example of the importance of communication came from a mafia boss.

It seems some years ago the authorities were after this mafia boss and they could never catch him because he protected his communication. He was very protective of the different ways he communicated. For instance, his accountant for a long time was a man who could not hear or speak. This made the boss feel better because it would be very hard to testify in court. But one day he realized he was missing $3,000,000 and he felt the accountant had taken it. He called the accountant into his office, and because he could not communicate with the accountant he had to use a sign language interpreter. The conversation went something like this:

> The mafia boss said to the interpreter, "You tell him I'm missing three million dollars and I know he's got it and I want it right now." The interpreter turns to the accountant and signs "He said he's missing three million dollars; he thinks you have it and he wants it right now." The account begins to sign back, "Tell him I'm a trusted loyal employee, I don't know what he's talking about, he must look somewhere else." The mafia boss is watching and says to the interpreter, "What'd he say." The interrupter relays the message to the mafia boss, and the mafia boss gets impatient, pulls a big gun out of his desk drawer, puts it to the accountants head, and says, "You tell him I know he's got my money and I want it right now or I'll blow his brains out." The interpreter turns to the accountant and says, "He is very upset, he says you have his money and if you don't give to him right now he'll blow your brains out." The account turns to the interpreter and starts flashing signs in hyper speed, "Tell him the money is under my mattress at my cabin by the lake." The mafia boss is watching these hands and he says to the interpreter, "What'd he say, what'd he say? The interpreter turns

to the mafia boss and says, "He said he doesn't think you have enough guts to pull the trigger!"

The moral of this story is we do not want to be misinterpreted. Therefore, if we want to be effective in communicating to others, our communication must be congruent. Let me have you consider something that is just as important, if not more important than communicating to others, and that is communicating to yourself. The greatest person you can talk to every day is yourself.

When you talk to yourself, your communication must also be congruent. You may lie to others but you cannot lie to yourself. Your brain knows when you're lying. You may say the right words but if your voice and body language doesn't line up, it will never become a "must do" in your life and it will never come to reality. Scripture confirms what I'm trying to tell you. In Mark chapter four Jesus explains that our words are seeds that we sow and our heart is the ground in which we sow them. In Matthew chapter twelve, Jesus says that it is out of the abundance of the heart that the mouth speaks. He says the good or bad treasure (seeds) that we plant in our heart is what we will experience in our life.

I could spend pages trying to explain this principle but you can read the Bible for yourself. If you're really interested in learning more, Mr. Ron McIntosh goes into great detail about the mind-heart connection and can provide you with a greater understanding into the things we physically control that affects our success. His material on "*Living a Life Without Limits,*" can be obtained by calling or writing his offices at 2805 E. 89th St. Tulsa, OK, 74137. I encourage everyone to get this information, study it for yourself, and start experiencing a change in your life.

One of the greatest examples that gave me the insight to practice this principle came years ago from Mr. Zig Ziglar when I heard him state, "Your input will determine your outlook, and your outlook will determine your output and your output will determine your destiny." He then went on

43

to prove the principle by telling a personal experience that took place in Birmingham, Alabama. He was scheduled to give a presentation in Birmingham and before the date of the event a woman called his office and asked if she could meet with him. She explained that she needed his help. He said he would meet with her before the presentation.

Mr. Ziglar explains the event like this: Upon his arrival they met and when he asked, "What can I do for you?" she replied, "I've got a problem with that place where I work." Mr. Ziglar said, "What is the problem?" She quickly stated in no uncertain terms, "I hate it, I hate everything about it, I hate the people, I hate the location, I hate what we do, I hate everything." Mr. Ziglar said, "I think I can help you," and she replied, "I knew you could, that's why I wanted to see you." He said "this is what you do, when you get home tonight, take a sheet of paper and write down everything you love about your job and your company." She immediately interrupted him and said, "I just told you I hate everything about it." He said, "You must do this" and then he made her take a sheet of paper right then and he began to ask her questions.

First question, "Do they pay you down there?" She replied, "Yes." He said, "You mean you'd rather work without pay?" She said, "No, that's silly." He said, "Write it down, I love my job because they pay me."

Second question, "Do they pay you average, above average or below average?" She replied, "I guess they pay me a little above average." He said, "You mean you'd rather be paid below average?" she quickly said, "No, that's silly." He said, "Write it down, I love my job because they pay me a little above average."

Third question, "Do they provide you a good place to work?" She replied, "Yes, I have a nice office." He said, "You mean you'd rather work out in the heat, rain, sleet, and snow?" She replied, "No, that's silly." He said, "Write it down, I love my job because they provide me a good place to work."

Mr. Ziglar went on to name twenty-two things she loved about her job and company. He asked her to do something and she committed to do it. He said, "Every night before you go to bed you recite these twenty-two things we've documented. Every morning when your feet hit the floor you recite these twenty-two things and in thirty days call me and we'll talk."

Thirty days went by and he didn't hear from her. About six weeks later he was back in Birmingham doing another presentation. About half way through his first session, he noticed the same lady sitting on the front row and she was smiling from ear to ear. At the first break he went down and asked, "Tell me how it's going down at work." She replied, "Mr. Ziglar, you wouldn't believe how those people down there have changed!" She did not realize what she did was change her input which changed her outlook, or perception, and her outlook changed her output, or action, which changed her future.

The truth is you don't have more problems than other people – you just think about them more often! Take a moment and consider what you just read. What you think about produces how you feel. If you don't believe that, try getting angry without first having angry thoughts, or getting sad without first having sad thoughts. You can not do it. To experience a feeling you must first have a thought that produces it. If you change how you think, you'll change how you feel!

Nothing can hold your negative feelings in place other than your own thinking. Once you understand that, you can get on the path to happiness. But change doesn't happen instantly. Negative thinking didn't appear overnight, and changing to positive thinking will not either. It takes time. Start by treating your negative thoughts in the same way you treat flies at a picnic, shoo them away and replace them with thoughts that are "excellent and praiseworthy."

Dr. Joyce Brothers says, "You cannot consistently perform in a manner that is inconsistent with the way you see yourself." Self-image is vital to having a positive attitude and proper self-communication is critical to building a proper self-image. As I've already stated, "You can't expect others to believe that you are skilled, talented, beautiful, sexy and successful until you believe it, and you're not going to believe it until you start telling yourself." You need to get up every morning, look yourself in the mirror, and tell yourself what you want to see happen, what you will accomplish, and what you will have happen in your life and body. Until you start telling yourself positive, uplifting, motivating and inspiring things you'll never experience the reality you want out of life.

Most successful people like to control events, but we can't control all events, can we? For example, let's take my father dying. I couldn't control it, but I could control what it meant to me. When you control what things mean, you control the secret to life, the quality of life for you.

When I received the assignment to the Middle East, Charlotte cried for weeks. I had been to that part of the world before; I had written home many times, and stated that anywhere in the world would be better to live than there.

After a few weeks of this type behavior, I realized we were on a road to disaster. I began to read more about how to control my life and how to get where I wanted by communicating better. This is when I was introduced to the material produced by great people like Zig Ziglar, Tony Robbins, Earl Nightingale and many others. We began to practice a positive self-communication principle. After a few days, we began to see the future differently; we began to discover the opportunities that were going to be possible. We started encouraging each other about how we would grow from this fantastic experience. Charlotte and I began to realize just how important this would be to the future of our three sons. To make a long story short, this was the best time of our lives. We gained more insight and knowledge of our own faith; we gained friends, achieved goals and began to experience the wonderful results of living life to its fullest.

I had many people over the years ask us how we went about changing our communication, and why it worked so well for us. I learned that by asking questions, I could change my thinking. As Mr. Ziglar says, "When you change your thinking, you change your action and when you change your action, you change your destiny." Changing thinking is only accomplished by changing your communication to yourself.

I did it by asking myself two questions about everything that happens, every event, and every situation I encounter every day. The first question is, what is great about this? As humans we automatically want to acknowledge the negative side of everything, but you must force yourself to answer the question. I have found there is always something great about everything. When you begin to do this, it initiates the positive thinking process which is extremely important to our success. The second question is, what can I do to make it better? Again, you must force yourself to answer the question. When you do, it will ignite the creative thinking process which will reinforce the positive thinking process.

Once you start this question and answer process, you will begin to see things from a different perspective. You'll see things from a more positive perspective, which changes how you not only look at things, but how you respond as well. We all know that success in life is not what happens, but how you respond to what happens. After disciplining yourself to do this for a month or more, it becomes habit and you do it without thinking, making it part of who you are.

Several years ago my brother-in-law, Lee, and his dad, were traveling to Kentucky to see his oldest son, who attended Sanford University, play football. They were hit by another vehicle from behind which caused their vehicle to go off the interstate and flip many times. It was a serious accident and when we arrived in the emergency room at Erlanger Medical Center, Lee was still on the stretcher with blood from head to toe. As he lay there, he was in and out of consciousness, but when he was conscious he was talking positive. Even at the scene of the accident, a doctor had come upon the scene and was reassuring Lee, as he lay on the pavement, that everything was going to be fine. He said Lee looked up at him and asked, "What kind of doctor are you?" He replied, "I'm a dentist" to which Lee replied, "I don't think anything is wrong with my teeth." The doctor said he was being extremely positive about everything.

The next morning, in the Intensive Care Unit, Lee looked at my sister and said, "Dad didn't make it did he?" She said, "No he didn't, but the doctors said he never knew what happened and he didn't feel any pain." His reply made me stop and review what I knew about his life. I had known Lee from grammar school and from then until now, he has always been well respected and successful. He is a brilliant business man, loving father, and faithful husband. His statement let me know why he is who he is. He looked at my sister and said, "If I had to pick a day for my dad to go, it would be a day like we had yesterday, full of fun and joy. If I could have picked a way for him to depart this world it would be just as he did, after a long, successful, meaningful life, with no pain and no suffering." If only more of us could have this outlook on life. To always be searching for the good in everything that happens and everyone we come in contact with.

Mastering communication is everything and we have the power to do so. We have the ability to decide what equals pain and what equals pleasure. Instead, we sometimes act like dogs. We let other people tell us how to feel and act. They say Americans watch television an average of seven hours a day. Even with the internet, CDs, and DVDs. What are we doing? We're allowing someone else to tell us what to feel and how to act.

A good example is television commercials. Advertisers can get you excited about dog food, chewing gum, automobiles, and many other things. They know how to condition you to feel certain ways to get you passionate about certain things. Statistics show that we must see or hear something at least seven times before we will respond to it. We are letting others set what psychologists call anchors in our mind. We can set our own anchors if we will just take the time and plant the proper things into our brain. The old saying, "if you don't like the output, change the input" is correct. Begin today to program yourself by communicating the right message to yourself.

OVERCOMING

6

OVERCOMING

"The Principle of Attitude"

The greatest resource on earth for you to achieve your goals is other people. Therefore, it's important to realize that your actions, feelings and moods will determine the actions, feelings and moods of others. It's your attitude that tells them what you expect in return. If you have a cheerful, expectant attitude it says to everyone you come in contact with that you expect the best in your dealings with the world.

After serving 21 years in the U.S. Air Force, working with pilots and around aircraft, I believe the example John Maxwell gives in his book, *The Winning Attitude*, is a perfect example of the most important thing that directs our lives and builds rapport with others. He explains that an airplane has many instruments that tell a pilot how the plane is operating, as well as the location and altitude. The instrument relied on greatly is called an "Attitude" indicator. This device indicates the position of the airplane in relation to the horizon. If the plan has a nose high attitude, the plane is climbing upward. If the nose is below the horizon, it is a low attitude meaning the craft is falling or descending. He says, "Even aircraft are driven by using attitude. Attitude

51

living is like attitude flying, it indicates our performance and direction."

We all want good results from life, in our home, in our work, and in all our contacts with other people. The most important single factor that guarantees good results, day in and day out, month after month, year after year, is a healthy attitude! "Attitude IS everything."

John Maxwell goes on to give some great definitions of attitude. He says attitude is:
- The "advance man" of our true selves.
- It is our best friend or our worst enemy.
- It is an outward look based on past experiences.
- It is a thing that draws people to us or repels them.
- It is the Librarian of our past, the Speaker of our present, the Prophet of our future.

Attitude is really a mental focus on the outside world based on past experiences. We expect certain things, and we tend to live out our expectations. Others give us what we expect. You see, our attitude is something we can control. We can establish our attitude each morning when we wake. Actually, we do just that, whether we realize it or not, and the whole world reflects back to us the attitude we present to them. It's our attitude toward life that determines life's attitude toward us.

It is a cause and effect principle. Everything we say or do will cause a corresponding effect. That is why you and I determine the quality of our own lives. We get back what we give out.

If you want to evaluate the quality of your past attitude; think about how people have reacted to you. Did they greet you with a smile, have a positive manner, and give you friendly greetings when you appeared? That should tell the story! And if you're not pleased, then you may need to do a check-up from the neck up.

Most people never think about their attitude. For most, it is just a matter of beginning each day in neutral. They wait to react to whatever situation they encounter. If the situation is good, they react well; if it's bad, they reflect that too. We can't wait to react to situations or circumstances; we must begin to control our own attitude. A person with a poor attitude toward learning, for example, isn't going to learn very much. You can probably think of examples in your own life. Or if you take the attitude you can't do something, you generally will not do it. If you think you can, or you think you can't – you're right!

There are millions of people today who live narrow, darkened, frustrated lives – who live defensively – simply because they take a defensive, doubtful attitude toward themselves and, as a result, toward life in general. A person with a poor attitude is a magnet for unpleasant experiences. And when those experiences come, they tend to reinforce the poor attitude, which brings problems, and more problems, and so on. It becomes a self-generating prophecy. Believe it or not, it's all based on attitude. We get what we expect.

In *What to Say When You Talk to Yourself*, Dr. Shad Hemstetter tells us we were told "no," or what we could not do, 148,000 times before age 18. If you couple that with our instantaneous access to all the negative happenings in the world, it's no wonder that leading behavioral researchers say as much as 77% of our thoughts are negative and counter-productive. Here's the good news – Dr. William James, the founder of modern psychology, stated way back in 1900, "The greatest discovery of my generation is that human beings may alter their lives by altering their attitudes of mind."

Let me share a perfect example of how a positive attitude can affect the success of a person. An organization in Nashville, Tennessee had an office in Tullahoma, Tennessee that had never been successful. In fact, the director of operations decided to fire the last two agents in the Tullahoma office and close the office down.

After several months, the director gets the idea that he can make someone successful if he can instill an optimistic perspective and a positive attitude in the person he hired for that office. He sold his idea to the head of the division after which he called a company meeting that included every person in the organization. At that meeting, he told them of his plan to re-open the Tullahoma office and that he needed their help in making it successful. He went on to explain how they would be involved in helping. He said, "Every time you speak to the person I hire, leave that person with the impression that the Tullahoma office has more potential than any in the organization. Tell him, you don't know how he got such a great office, you wanted that office. All he needs to do to be successful is just show up for work." He received full participation because no one wanted to experience his wrath.

As you can imagine, everyone agreed and he went looking for a candidate. It wasn't long before he found and hired the person. On the first day, at orientation the new hire was approached by the trainer and asked, "How did you get that office in Tullahoma? I wanted that office, I was willing to go back out into production to get that office, that location has more potential than any in the state, people down there love our organization."

Every time the new hire talked to another branch or to someone at headquarters, they left him with the impression he had one of the greatest opportunities in the entire organization. Even when he was having a bad month they would tell him, "You better hang on to your seat because a bad month for you means you'll triple next month." He never saw failure.

You can guess what happened. He was 150% of his goal the first year. The second year he was over 200%. He was winning awards, contests and having fun working with people. After the third year, at the annual awards banquet, he was winning most of the yearly awards and it was then that the director of operations decided it was safe to tell how this happened. After the awards, he steps to the podium and begins to tell the story. I was sitting about four tables back and I became very upset because I was the one he hired. I thought to myself, "I've been manipulated; these guys have given me a worthless office and expected me to make it work."

After a few minutes, I really began to see it differently. What they had done was teach me a life principle. If I could maintain a positive attitude and outlook, I could be successful doing almost anything, anywhere, anytime. However, it was almost ten years later after working for a very powerful and influential person, who taught me even more about what I wanted out of life, that I discovered how to build and maintain a positive attitude. We don't all work in a perfect environment, around perfect people, who will give such encouraging feedback in order to build such a great attitude, but it can be done. We do it through self-communication. I must tell myself what I want to see happen in my life, and I must do it day after day after day. Only then will it begin to manifest in my life.

It's hard sometimes to convince people that the world they experience is a reflection of their attitude. They tend to take the attitude that if people would be nice to them, they would be nice in return. It's like sitting in front of a cold stove waiting on the heat, but the heat isn't coming until we put fuel in the stove. I believe the Bible says it best, "Do unto others as you would have them do unto you." It's up to us to act first, it has to start somewhere. Let it start today!

Our attitude is a reflection of who we are inside. Think about the people who go through life, from one success to another, and when they do fail at something, they just shrug it off and head right out again.

It doesn't matter what people do, wherever you find people doing an outstanding job and getting great results, you'll find people with a positive attitude. These people take the attitude that they can accomplish whatever they set out to accomplish. They take the attitude that achievement is the natural order of things (and it is). They take the attitude that there is no reason why they can not be as successful and competent as anyone else. They have a healthy attitude toward themselves and as a result, toward life and the things they want to accomplish.

Here is a large part of the problem with some people today. They have a poor attitude toward themselves. They must change the picture they have of themselves before attempting to change their attitude toward life.

It starts with what we allow to be fed into our minds. We are told most of our life how things will not work, what our limitations are, and for some, just how incompetent they are mentally. This builds a picture in the mind of who you are, what you can accomplish, and what you should not even attempt. Psychologists say by the time we graduate high school, we have fixed the set points in our mind of what we can and cannot accomplish in life. However, most everyone can change these set points through gaining knowledge and positive self-communication.

As I shared in an earlier chapter, Dr. Joyce Brothers says, "You cannot consistently perform in a manner that is inconsistent with the way you see yourself." You are "fearfully and wonderfully made." Be proud of it and use what your Creator has given you for this life. A recent study sited by Focus on the Family radio broadcast stated that the number one reason for a poor self image is the "lack of unconditional love." Everyone wants and needs to be loved. We can, and we must, express love to those we encounter, especially those closest to us. The number two reason sited was "the things programmed into our mind by others." The world starts programming failure into us at birth. While we should respect the opinions of others, we should never let their negative outlook infiltrate our attitude. If you let it, the criticism of others will steal your individuality, rob you of your creativity, and stop you from fulfilling your destiny.

It takes practice and time to re-program our thinking before we begin to see ourselves as brilliant, successful, talented, and beautiful. We must start putting the right images into our mind. We must begin sowing the right words into our heart. We will then begin to take a different view of ourselves. When we change our thinking, we change our action; and when we change our action, we change our future.

To change the image we have of ourselves, we must start by changing some things around us. First, don't be a garbage disposal for others who want to spread negative, depressing, immoral thoughts. Surround yourself with upbeat, motivated, and enthusiastic people. Now, this may be hard, especially if you are married to someone who is the opposite of what you are trying to achieve. But, I believe you can change them as you change yourself; it just takes determination, commitment, and persistence. Use outside sources to feed yourself and bring them home.

Second, talk to intelligent people, especially yourself. The best person you can talk to everyday is yourself. Be positive, motivated and enthusiastic. Tell yourself how great you are; if you don't believe it, others sure won't think it! Be like the old man who talked to himself continually. When asked why he talked to himself he replied, "For two reasons, first I like to talk to intelligent people; second, I like to hear intelligent people talk." There is nothing wrong with his self-image is there?

Once you change the input to your mind, you begin to see yourself with a more positive attitude; therefore, your outlook on life begins to change for the better. You start to become the person you think you are, have more of the things you desire, and accomplish the things you set out to accomplish.

It is impossible to even estimate the number of jobs that are lost, promotions missed, sales ruined, or marriages that fail all because of poor attitudes. We can not even count the millions of jobs that are held but hated; the marriages that are tolerated but unhappy; the parents and children who fail to understand and love one another – all because of a poor attitude. They don't understand that what they're getting is a reflection of themselves. Nothing can change until you do.

So, how do you develop a good positive attitude? The same way we develop other abilities: through practice! Most of us need to put a sign on the bathroom mirror that simply reads "ATTITUDE." That way, we'll see it first thing in the morning and be reminded to check it and put it in gear to get the most out of the day. It may also help us to smile, speak to people and reach out to people more.

Everything we want to do or get done, we must do with and through people. Every dollar we will ever earn will come from other people. The person we love, and with whom we want to spend the rest of our life, is a human being with whom we must interact. Our children are individuals, each different from anyone ever born. What affects them most is our attitude – the loving kindness they see and feel whenever we are around them.

Someone once said, "Life is dull only to dull people." It's true! It's also true that life is interesting only to interesting people, and life is successful only to successful people. We must be the epitome of success. We must radiate success before it will come to us. We must first become mentally, from an attitude standpoint, the people we wish to become physically and socially.

Many years ago, a newspaper reporter asked a famous Los Angeles businessman, "When did you become successful?" He replied, "I was successful when I was dead broke. I knew what I wanted to do, and I knew I'd do it. It was only a matter of time." He had a successful attitude long before the success he sought had become a reality. The great German philosopher and writer, Johann Wolfgang Von Goethe, put it this way: "Before you can do something, you must be something."

Let me give you a simple guide given to the world by Earl Nightingale in his training series *"Leading the Field."*

He says to "Treat every person with whom you come in contact as the most important person on earth." He says you do that for three reasons: 1) As far as every person is concerned, they are the most important person on earth; 2) That is the way human beings should treat each other, and 3) By treating everyone this way, we begin to form an important habit. This habit will draw people and open doors of opportunity that can change your future.

There's nothing in the world that men, women and children want and need more than self-esteem – the feeling that they're important, they're recognized, and needed, they count and are respected. They will give their love, respect and their business to the person who fills this need.

Treat the members of your family as the very important people they are, the most important people in the world. Each morning, carry out into the world the kind of attitude you'd have if you were the most successful person on earth. Notice how quickly it develops into a habit. Almost immediately, you'll notice a change. Irritations that used to frustrate you will begin to disappear. Also when some less-informed person gives you a bad time, you will not let their poor attitude infect yours.

Destructive emotions, such as anger, hatred, and jealousy, don't hurt others; they hurt you. They can make your life miserable. They can make you sick. Forgive everyone who ever hurt you – really forgive them – and then forgive yourself. That is all in the past. Stewing over a situation or past hurt can only make you sick. Forgive and forget. Get rid of it. You have risen above that self-destructive behavior.

Whoever coined the cliché "Life's too short" certainly knew what they were talking about. It really is too short – much too short – to spend any of our valuable time mimicking the attitudes of others – unless they are good attitudes. The greatest tragedy that could happen would be to grow old and realize that somewhere along the way you lost yourself, and never succeeded at being the person you were designed to be. That is a distinct possibility if you allow the opinions and attitudes of others to rule your life. Great attitudes do much more than turn on the lights in our worlds; they seem to magically connect us to all sorts of unexpected opportunities that were somehow absent before the change. Maybe that's what people mean when they say "you're lucky." It's really nothing more than a new outlook that comes with a great attitude.

When you begin to develop a positive attitude, you are placing yourself among the top 5% of the people – among the most successful people on earth. You've placed yourself on the road to what you seek.

VISION

7

VISION

"The Principle of Goal Setting"

Some people act like they're going to wake up one morning and "poof" they've arrive with all the things they desire. The fact is that vision without action is just a daydream, and action without vision is a nightmare. We must follow through with discipline in our lives if we expect to accomplish anything. People who succeed in life and business today have a pattern of how they do it. They follow what some call the fundamental laws of success.

Everyone who achieves their goals does so by taking specific steps. Setting goals is as essential to achieving what you want out of life, as food is to sustaining and growing your body.

It is said that Howard Hill was one of the best archers in the world. He entered 273 tournaments and he finished first in all 273. He shot a Bengal Tiger, Cape buffalo and was the first to kill a Rhino without a rifle backup. But, if you blindfolded Howard Hill and spin him around 15 times he couldn't hit anything. You may say, "How could he hit a target he can't see?" However, I have a better question, "How can you hit a target you don't have?" You "must" set goals.

The first step to going anywhere or achieving anything is to know what you really want. You must know the outcome you are expecting to achieve. This is called a goal. The clearer you can become about what you want, the more power you'll have to achieve it.

You cannot decide what to deal with today, unless you know where you want to be tomorrow. Any plan to improve your use of time depends on being clear about your goals. The Scriptures read, *"Make a decree and it will be established..., write the vision down and make it plain."* If it worked 3,000 years ago, it will work for you and me today. When you discipline yourself to do the things you need to do, when you need to do them, the day is going to come when you can do the things you want to do, when you want to do them.

Bobby Knight, head basketball coach and winner of several national championships at Indiana University, accurately states that "The will to win is nothing without the will to prepare to win." He is right! However, before we can plan, we must decide what we want out of life. So let me ask you, "What do you want?"

Most people start with how much money they want to earn or save. I'll be the first to agree that money is important, it rates right up there with oxygen; you cannot live without it. But money is not the most important thing in our lives. We must look at where we want to end up in life. Remember your purpose? Setting goals centers around your purpose. Keep in mind that it's not where you start; it's where you go that makes the difference.

Up until a few years ago, I bought into a theory that says "You are where you are because that's where you want to be." I taught it and believed it. Then I realized how false that statement really was. You are where you are because of several factors; you've either been advised by parents, professors, or peers or driven by situations, circumstances, or desire; or led by present and past leaders and authority

63

figures you trusted and admired. But, you don't have to stay where you are.

A report published many years ago in Forbes magazine revealed that entrepreneurs who made money did so after they moved to a new city. Let me point out that some made their money when they moved from Boston to Chicago. However, others made their money when they moved from Chicago to Boston, some when they moved from Dallas to Denver and still those that moved from Denver to Dallas.

The point is the city was not the determining factor. "When they moved they planned to make money in their new location. They prepared to make money, and, therefore expected to make money. Not only that, but they made a commitment to make money there. However, you don't have to leave your current position to plan, prepare, expect, and commit. You can plan, prepare, expect, and make the commitment right where you are, doing exactly what you're doing.

A study conducted by Dr. David Jensen revealed that people who set goals and develop an action plan earn an average of $4,000 per month more than those who don't. That's why only 3% of all Americans finish life with most of the things money will buy and all the things money won't buy. They set goals that are designed to reap the most benefit from life itself. But why do most people reject or fail to set goals?

The first reason is fear. Fear makes procrastinators and cowards of us all. Fear and a poor self-image are almost, if not impossible, to separate. Direction can drive out fear if we use it correctly.

For example, if we take a trip from Dallas, Texas to Washington, D.C. with no directions, maps, or signs, we would have a certain degree of fear. But with directions, good maps, and road signs, our fear would greatly decrease. Actually, very few of us would attempt such a trip without directions and/or maps. Unfortunately, very few people are equipped with specific directions on how to navigate the highways of life. That is why people end up at the end of life's journey with just a fraction of what life has to offer.

Dr. Karl A. Menninger of Harvard University said, "Fears are educated into us and can, if we wish, be educated out." James Allen, author of *As a Man Thinketh*, stated, "He who has conquered doubt and fear has conquered failure."

The second reason people do not set goals is that they have never been convinced they needed them. Years ago when I first saw Dr. Jensen's study, I was convinced that I needed to start a personal goals program because a $4,000 per month increase was important. Creating and following a personal goals program instantly gave me 10 more hours each week. Can you use an additional 10 hours per week? That's 520 hours a year or 65 working days. How much can you accomplish with 65 more days each year?

I know you're still hung up on the $4,000 more per month. Most people who read this or listen to my presentations think, "My boss or company will never pay me $4,000 more per month." That is were you must start to change your thinking. I believe that every person should have four streams of income into their life. Most have them, they just haven't developed them to the point they are paying what they need to pay. Also, everyone has skills, talents, gifts and abilities that could be used to bring income into their life. But again, they haven't developed them or recognized their potential to use them for increase. This point alone would take a book to explain. Start today to identify your gifts, talents, and skills and see how they could benefit you more in the future.

I hope you understand and see, based on the evidence, that if we are to become successful, it is imperative that we use our time wisely, and that means getting started on a goals program.

The third reason most don't have a personal goals program is they don't know how to develop one. Let me briefly show you how to start. First, I recommend getting

Zig Ziglar's book, *Over the Top*, it outlines specifically, every step needed to complete your personal goals program. There are actually several good books and courses you can take to help in setting up a good goals program for yourself, but none compare with Mr. Ziglar's.

To be fair, there is good news and bad news in initiating a goals program. The bad news is properly developing a goals program will take several hours. A goals program is demanding, which is one of the reasons only 3% of us have one. The thought of investing the time might be overwhelming, or you simply may not have time. Lack of time always has been, and always will be, the problem. The solution is to make the commitment to establish a goals program now, and then you will have more time in the future to do what you need and want to do.

The first thing is to make the commitment to take step one now, before you turn out the lights tonight. Remember! Change starts when you take the first step, and without action there will be no progress. The good news is, when you take the steps suggested you will create for yourself an additional two to ten hours of productive time every week for the rest of your life. When you learn how to set one goal, you will know how to set them all. Keep in mind that all your goals should be SMART goals – Specific, Measurable, Attainable, Realistic and Timely.

Let me very briefly go through some of the steps that Mr. Ziglar recommends in his book. This is no substitute for his book, I recommend getting Mr. Ziglar's book to help you fully understand and complete each step.

First, write down on a sheet of paper everything you want to be, everything you want to do, everything you want to obtain, and why you want it. Let your imagination run wild; be sure to include your family in this process.

Next, put the paper aside for a day or two. Then come back and answer the question why you would like to accomplish each item you have printed on your Idea Sheet. If you can't express in one sentence why you want to be, do, or have it, eliminate it as a current goal. Remember, this list is probably far too many things to work on every day. You will have to temporarily eliminate most of them so you can concentrate on those that are important right now.

Take time to answer some questions about your goals, all of which must have a yes answer. Is it really my goal or is it something someone else wants me to do? Is it morally right and fair to everyone concerned? If it's not legal, moral and ethical - forget it. Will reaching this goal take me closer to, or farther from, my purpose? Can I physically and emotionally commit myself to start and finish this goal? Can I visualize myself reaching this goal?

Also, ask yourself, will reaching this goal give me more joy, health, wealth, friends, peace of mind, security, improve family relationships, and hope? And most importantly, will reaching these goals contribute to a more balanced success in my life?

Divide the remaining goals into three categories: Short-range (one month or less), Intermediate (one month to one year), and Long-range (one year or more). Remember that some goals must be big or out of reach, but not out of sight. Others will be long-range to keep you on track. Some must be small and daily to make certain that you become, and remain, a person with a dream instead of a dreamer. Other goals will be ongoing.

Lastly, take the remaining goals and answer some additional questions related to the goal. Questions like, what are the benefits of reaching this goal? What obstacles will I have to overcome to reach this goal? What skills or knowledge are required to reach this goal? Who will I need to work with in order to reach this goal? What plan of action do I need to reach this goal? When do I need to complete this goal? Remember, some goals will be on-going and others will have a completion date.

The people with whom you share your goals will play a major part in whether or not you achieve them. Share give-up goals (smoking, weight loss, drinking etc.) freely. Share your go-up goals carefully. These goals should only be shared with individuals who will be inclined to be supporters and encouragers.

We now have briefly covered the first step in becoming successful. Let me continue with my statement in the beginning of this chapter covering the remaining laws of success.

The second thing successful people do is know why they want it. That's why the goals process is so important. You must know the purpose for achieving a goal. Until you know why you want something, you'll never have the power to accomplish whatever it takes to get it. When I say whatever it takes, I mean it must be legal, moral, and ethical. Many people obtain things other ways, but they fail to hold on to them because it was gained the wrong way.

The third thing successful people do is take massive action to accomplish their goal. They devise a strategy and start moving toward the goal. Let me ask you a question. What would cause someone who knows what they want and why they want it, to never take action? The number one answer is fear. What is fear? A very good friend of mine told me a few years ago that fear is "False Evidence Appearing Real." That is very true. Most of the things we fear, we have no reason to fear them other than what we allowed to be built up in our mind, either by our environment or others around us.

Every psychologist in the world will tell you the greatest way to overcome fear is with physiology, or simply stepping out in the face of fear. When you step out in the face of fear, you begin to increase your courage and start the process of realizing that fears can not hold you back if you are determined and committed to your action.

Let me give you a personal example. In 1989, I was serving on a Foreign Military Sales Team stationed in Amman, Jordan. In the later part of July, I was working in a little place called Azraq. It is located on the northeast border of Jordan near Iraq and Syria. As I finished my work late that afternoon, I started back to my home in Amman. As I traveled a few miles on what is known as the King's Highway (which stretches from Baghdad, Iraq to Amman, Jordan), I came upon hundreds of tanks and personnel carriers with what looked like thousands of Iraqi troops.

Fear gripped me because I knew the Iraqis I had encountered in the past didn't like Americans very much; I'm in an American car. I began to assess the situation; I was driving an armored Chevrolet Impala, and I had a nine millimeter pistol. They had tanks; there wouldn't have been enough of me left to prove I was even in the country, if they so chose.

The first thing that came to mind was, do something. After working in Middle Eastern countries for several years, I remembered that everyone loved to communicate, even with those they weren't fond of. I started waving my hands and yelling, even though they couldn't hear through the bullet proof windows, "HELLO! HELLO!"

After about 30 seconds of waving and yelling, they started to wave back to me. As they did the tanks and personnel carriers started parting the way so I could drive between them. I'm convinced that I made it through that situation because I took action and did something physically. Even though I wasn't able to wear those pants again, I did make it through by taking physical action. Never let fear stop you!

The fourth thing successful people do to achieve success is measure their progress. They know what they are getting. It is important to recognize that when you're not moving toward what you want, change your approach. You may be running east with total physical intensity looking for a sunset, but you're never going to see it. So you must stop and change direction or change your approach to what you're doing.

How many times must you change your approach before moving toward your goal? Some people try things once, twice or maybe even three times and quit. Because they say, "I don't want to look like a fool, or I'm never going to try that again, it'll never work." You must take the same attitude as a young mother trying to get her baby to walk. If you ask how long are you going to try to get your baby to walk before you give it up? She'll tell you, "Never, my baby is going to walk." The formula is the same for you and me. Never give up, keep changing your approach until you accomplish your goal.

If you study the life of Thomas Edison, you'll find a good example. It is said that he had 10,000 experiments before achieving the light bulb. I saw a documentary a while back that said at his 9,999[th] experiment, his best friend was in the lab with him, and the lab blew up. When the smoke cleared and the ash settled, his best friend stood up and saw Mr. Edison writing in his journal. His best friend said, "Are you going to have 10,000 failures before you give this stupid idea up?" Mr. Edison looked up and said, "I didn't have a failure, I just found 9,999 ways not to invent the light bulb. However, I did discover how to make a small explosion, which might be helpful in the future." He never gave up; he kept changing his approach until he got what he wanted.

Another great example is Bruce Springsteen. Do you think he just jumped on stage one day and became "The Boss?" Bruce said he went to hundreds of agents and they all told him the same thing, "Bruce, just play the guitar and keep your mouth shut, no one wants to hear you sing." Did he quit, NO! He kept changing his approach until he got what he wanted. That's why he's called "The Boss" today.

Before we end this chapter and this book, let me ask you a very important question. If I were to give you $86,400 and told you to spend all of it today, that you could carry none over to tomorrow, you must spend it all because tomorrow you will receive another $86,400, how would you spend it?

That is TIME. You get 86,400 seconds each day to do with what you wish. The question is how are you spending it? Time is a funny thing, when it's gone, it's really gone, and we can never regain any of it. The late Adrian Rogers said, "The misuse of anything as precious as time should be a crime. If somebody steals your car...you can acquire another. If they snatch your wallet...a few phone calls would salvage the majority of your concerns. But who can you call when you lose your time?" If time is money, then we really need to make it work for us to reach our goals in life. That's why so many people are living beneath their desires; they haven't properly used their time. I've heard many people say at the end of their life, if they could do it over again they'd spend their time better, and they would put more emphasis on the things that matter. I was told once that I should set my priorities based on who would be crying at my funeral, which was very was good advice.

Time is our most valuable resource. People's attitudes toward time are complex and inconsistent. If you want to use your time efficiently to accomplish all that you need to do at work and at home, you need to take a closer look at the habits and attitudes that shape your use of time. That is why setting goals are so important.

The meaning and importance of time is different depending on the culture. I think one of the most common obstacles people face in managing their days lies in the way they view time. Therefore, the very first step in taking control of time is to challenge your very perception of it.

Most people think of time as intangible. In the journey from chaos to order, it is often easier to organize space than time because space is something you can actually see. Time, on the other hand, is completely invisible. You can't touch it, it doesn't pile up, and you can't hold it in your hand. So we need to change our perception of time and develop a more tangible view of it. We need to learn to see time in more visual, measurable terms.

It is very sobering to calculate exactly how much your time costs and then realize how much of it is not being spent efficiently. If you want to see how valuable your time is to your employer use the following formula.

Multiply your annual salary by 1.5 – to include over head
And divide the total by the number of working hours in a year
Divide this total by 60.

$$\frac{1.5 \text{ x annual salary}}{\text{Working hours per year}} = \text{Cost per hour}$$

$$\frac{\text{Cost per hour}}{60} = \text{Cost per minute}$$

Now think about a few of the tasks you have to do and calculate how much it cost you to do those tasks. Think about the ways you can better perform those tasks or delegate them. Is it worth your cost or should you give them to someone junior. It's a matter of cost. Therefore, we need to set aside time each day to review and prioritize demands on our time.

Use your time wisely. We all should be aware of the cost of time. We as individuals and organizations are held accountable for our use of time. Goals are defined and financial penalties are incurred for missed deadlines. Each week, month, and year we have new goals to reach in our job. We don't think about it, but the same should occur in our personal life. We should have goals, some weekly, monthly, and yearly.

Let me also say we should make a point to value other people's time. I've had appointments with individuals who were not ready when I arrived, making me have to wait. The medical community seems to be the worst. I know it's hard to schedule accurately in such a challenging environment, but to make someone wait three or four hours for a thirty minute appointment is excruciating.

Too many organizations and departments have defined working hard with working long hours and that's not necessarily so. It's been proven that long hours often decrease efficiency and productivity. Ways of using your time become habitual, so we must make an initial investment of time to re-think and improve our habits. Todd Duncan points out in his book, *Time Traps*, that success in any endeavor is a result of focused time. He reminds us that Rocky went to the mountains of Siberia to train for his fight with Ivan Drago. Alejandro Murrieta takes to a cave with his mentor to learn the ways of Zorro. Rannulph Junuh learns to "see the field" and gets his swing back. And Billy Chapel "closes the mechanism" and pitches a perfect game. To become great at anything, you have to learn to focus your time. The rewards will be the ability to control your workload, and have more time to focus on the most important aspects of your work and life.

You can start by identifying a small chunk of a difficult task, then deal with it right away. One of the greatest tools I use is a time log. I can split my working day into thirty minute blocks. When I first started using one, I was surprised at how much time I spent unproductively and how little time I spent working and planning. Using a time log gives you a starting point to assess areas for improvement. How long you should keep a time log is dependent on the nature of your work. If you work on a monthly cycle, keep it for a couple of months. If it is weekly, then 2-3 weeks should be enough.

According to Dr. John Maxwell, "If there is hope in the future, there is power in the present." Take the first step by putting into place the principles we shared in this book. Make decisions wisely; begin to use what you were designed with. Set higher standards for yourself; define your purpose. Let all your communication be positive (especially to yourself) which will allow you to build a good attitude and set goals for your life.

Remember, when you sow a thought, you reap an action; when you sow an action, you reap a habit; when you sow a habit, you reap a character; and when you sow a

73

character, you reap a destiny. It's not what happens to you, it's how you handle it that makes you a winner. Yesterday ended last night; today is a brand new day and the day is yours. Make it count!

SUMMARY

If you're serious about taking personal responsibility in developing excellence, then start today practicing these principles in your personal and professional life and watch what happens in a few short weeks. Begin now to make decisions based on how your future will be affected. Set higher standards for yourself; define your purpose, if you do not already know exactly what it is. Communicate the right message to yourself and build a positive attitude. Set goals and begin to measure your progress. Once you begin to see the results, you'll never turn back.

To really earn the top rewards, ask yourself what you want people to do for you; then grab the initiative and do it for them...give without expecting a return. I promise – you'll never – regret it. Love expecting nothing in return. Give, though they'll never say thanks. Forgive, even though they won't forgive you. Come early, stay late, and invest everything you've got even though nobody notices. It's a high calling to set such a standard for yourself! If you think some people are just naturally more loving than others, think again. Love is a choice – one that costs! You can't love others while you're staring into a mirror, or give to others while you're clinging to what you've got. Love will cost you your time, your money and your preoccupation with self. If you think you can just go to church some Sunday morning, read a book or attend a 7-step seminar and turn into a person of excellence – good luck! There are no pre-packaged programs or "add-and-stir" formulas to become a person of excellence. You must take personal responsibility in developing it through living the principles that will lead you to it.

ACKNOWLEDGEMENTS

New King James Bible/Thomas Nelson, Inc.

Over the Top, Zig Ziglar/Thomas Nelson Publishers

The Winning Attitude, John Maxwell/Thomas Nelson Publishers

Understanding Your Potential, Dr. Myles Munroe/Destiny Image

Time Management from the Inside Out, Julie Morgenstern/Owl Books

The Psychology of Winning, Denis Waitley/Nightingale-Conant

Lead the Field, Earl Nightingale/Nightingale-Conant

Unleashing the Power Within, Tony Robbins/Nightingale -Conant

Stories for the Heart, Alice Gray/Multnomah

Profiles in Faith, Harold Sala/Barbour Publishing

Cure for the Common Life, Max Lucado/W. Publishing Group

Standing for Light and Truth, Adrian Rogers/Crossways Books

Live Your Best Life Now, Joel Osteen/Warner Faith

Life Essentials, Tony Evans/Moody Publishers

Who You Are When No One's Looking, John Ortberg/Zondervan

Fields of God, Andy Stanley/Tyndale

Getting Through the Tough Stuff, Charles Swindoll/W. Publishing Group

Running with the Giants, John C. Maxwell/Warner Books

Time Traps, Todd Duncan/Nelson Business

OTHER BOOKS AVAILABLE

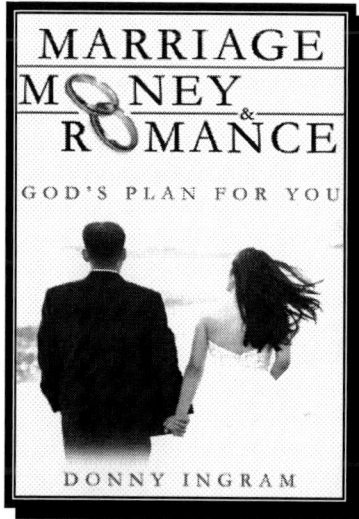

MARRIAGE
MONEY
&
ROMANCE

GOD'S PLAN FOR YOU

DONNY INGRAM

Marriage, Money & Romance is an outstanding guidebook for the marriage relationship. Anyone desiring to create and maintain a relationship filled with love, joy, dedication and commitment should read this book. It explains the roll of the husband, wife, parent and provider. It is a roadmap for singles looking to get married, newlyweds just getting started, or those who have been married for many years. It is a valuable resource for every home desiring a lifelong marriage that will produce health, wealth and happiness.

This book can be purchased from AuthorHouse Publishing, 1663 Liberty Drive, Suite 200 Bloomington, IN 47403, phone 888-519-5121, fax 812-349-0820. The publisher's online store can be viewed at www.authorhouse.com.

To speak to the author, schedule an interview, or speaking engagement please e-mail donny@ingrammanagement.com

ABOUT THE AUTHOR

Donny Ingram was born January 31, 1954, in Marianna, Florida to Billy Joe and Maxine Ingram. He was married to wife Charlotte in November, 1974, and they have raised three sons. Donny served over twenty years with the United States Air Force and finished his career at Air University in Montgomery, Alabama.

He is an author, motivational trainer, conference speaker and President of Ingram Management Group. For over twenty years, he has worked in sales and marketing, as well as training and development for both government and corporate America. Donny is responsible for the development of *"Recognizing Your Potential,"* a corporate training program that focuses on human design, communication, and attitude.

He and Charlotte are founders of *"Success in the Home,"* a marriage and family relationship training series. They have lived, worked and studied abroad with many different cultures and nationalities. Donny has a goal of helping people recognize their true potential and maximize their efforts in order to live life to its fullest.

MEMBER
NSA
NATIONAL SPEAKERS ASSOCIATION

To order more books or schedule a speaking/training engagement email <u>donny@ingrammanagement.com</u>